T0299665

The Sober Life Journal

FINDING FREEDOM ONE DAY AT A TIME

Simon Chapple

First published in Great Britain by Sheldon Press in 2022
An imprint of John Murray Press
A division of Hodder & Stoughton Ltd,
An Hachette UK company

1

A CIP catalogue record for this title is available from the British Library

Hardback ISBN 978 1 39 980429 5
eBook ISBN 978 1 39 980430 1

Typeset by KnowledgeWorks Global Ltd.

Printed and bound in Great Britain by Clays Ltd, Elcograf S.p.A.

John Murray Press policy is to use papers that are natural, renewable and recyclable products and made from wood grown in sustainable forests. The logging and manufacturing processes are expected to conform to the environmental regulations of the country of origin.

John Murray Press
Carmelite House
50 Victoria Embankment
London EC4Y 0DZ

Nicholas Brealey Publishing
Hachette Book Group
Market Place, Center 53, State Street
Boston, MA 02109, USA

www.sheldonpress.co.uk

Contents

Introduction

Let's find your freedom

We all want to experience a life where we enjoy calm, peace and happiness, where day-to-day frustrations aren't causing us emotional upset and we aren't thinking about drinking all the time.

Yet we live in a world where we are experiencing more stress and anxiety than ever before, greater demands are being placed on us, and it can be all too easy to end up feeling overwhelmed by the pressure and needing a drink to relax or detach from the world. This can lead to a cycle of behaviour that can feel impossible to break free from.

Why is an alcohol-free lifestyle so good?

Alcohol is poison – ethanol, to be precise. When we drink, it impacts negatively on our mind and body in many different ways. Alcohol has been linked to anxiety, depression and a range of other mental health problems, as well as being known to cause physical problems ranging from aches and pains to cancer.

On top of this, alcohol is addictive: when we drink, it activates the reward centre in our brain which makes us want more. Once we are in the loop of regular drinking, it can feel hard to escape.

Without alcohol in our lives we let go of the worries, the cravings and the negative effects of drinking. We find complete freedom, we become happier, feel calmer and start to make choices that align with our personal values.

Yet many people become stuck in their drinking because of their own false beliefs, because they firmly believe that alcohol provides some benefit and value in their lives.

What's the answer?

At the foundation of an alcohol-free life is self-awareness, which is the ability to notice how you feel, physically, emotionally, intellectually and spiritually. This awareness can be cultivated: it's just like learning a new skill and with practice you will soon be able to master it.

As your self-awareness develops, you will find yourself becoming curious about your beliefs and questioning how true they really are, and how much they are benefiting your life. It won't be long before you are forming new beliefs that leave you feeling empowered and aligned with the person you really are.

The sobriety movement has been growing quickly over recent times, and for hundreds of thousands of people around the world it has become a way of life that has seen them transform their levels of happiness and find complete freedom in the choices they make.

I want you to be part of this incredible movement. You can start right now by diving into the first few pages of this journal and learning something new about yourself.

How to use this journal

This journal has been created for anyone who wants to live an alcohol-free life. It doesn't matter whether you have been sober for many years or whether you are still drinking. All you need to do is make a commitment to spend a little time with your journal each day. Five to ten minutes daily will be enough.

Each day you will find self-explanatory reflections and exercises that will ensure you evolve into the best version of yourself. You will learn how to create a sobriety toolbox, develop your self-awareness, and understand how to meet your needs without alcohol. Above all, you will become stronger and committed to the choices you make about drinking.

Let's get started with your first day right now.

Simon Chapple
The Quit Alcohol Coach

Find more support, tips and advice at www.besober.co.uk

Date: ___/___/___

HOW WOULD YOU RATE TODAY?

☆ ☆ ☆ ☆ ☆

WRITE ABOUT YOUR DAY

TOP 3 THINGS ABOUT TODAY

1.

2.

3.

HOW HAVE YOU FELT TODAY?

WHAT INSPIRED YOU THE MOST TODAY?

3 INTENTIONS FOR TOMORROW

1.

2.

3.

YOUR REASON(S) FOR QUITTING ALCOHOL

Changing a habit like quitting drinking requires the right mindset. You can achieve this by having a strong reason or reasons for quitting. Create a reason why statement and refer back to it if you need a motivational boost.

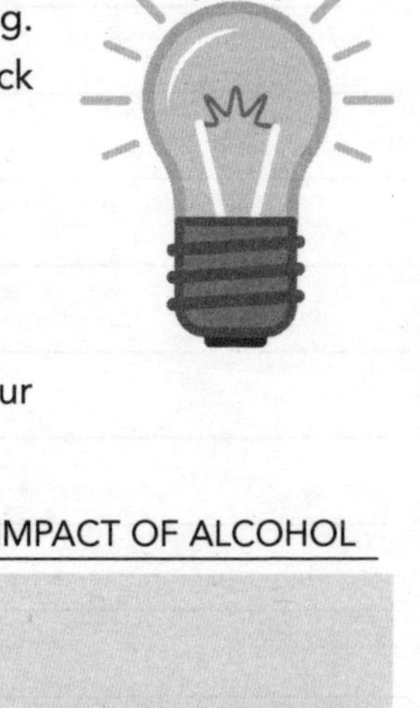

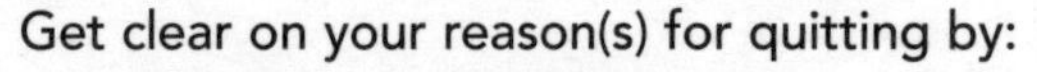

Get clear on your reason(s) for quitting by:

1. understanding what you will gain
2. knowing what you will lose
3. being clear on the impact of alcohol on your life and health.

WHAT WILL YOU GAIN?

NEGATIVE IMPACT OF ALCOHOL

WRITE DOWN YOUR REASON WHY STATEMENT

My primary reason to quit alcohol is:

Date: __/__/__

HOW WOULD YOU RATE TODAY?

☆☆☆☆☆

WRITE ABOUT YOUR DAY

TOP 3 THINGS ABOUT TODAY

1.

2.

3.

HOW HAVE YOU FELT TODAY?

WHAT INSPIRED YOU THE MOST TODAY?

3 INTENTIONS FOR TOMORROW

1.

2.

3.

WHAT HAVE YOU GOT TO LOSE?

List everything you hope to gain or achieve by quitting drinking. How motivated are you to receive the benefits of living an alcohol-free life?

How important is it to you to give up alcohol?

WHAT I HOPE TO GAIN IN MY LIFE BY QUITTING DRINKING

MY MOTIVATION LEVEL IS ____________________

(Low Medium High)

If your motivation is low or medium, what do you need to better prepare to quit drinking? I need:

1. ____________________
2. ____________________
3. ____________________
4. ____________________

Date: __/__/__

HOW WOULD YOU RATE TODAY?

WRITE ABOUT YOUR DAY

TOP 3 THINGS ABOUT TODAY

1.

2.

3.

HOW HAVE YOU FELT TODAY?

WHAT INSPIRED YOU THE MOST TODAY?

3 INTENTIONS FOR TOMORROW

1.

2.

3.

HOW WILL THIS TIME BE DIFFERENT?

The sober journey is unique for everyone.

Understanding what you need to succeed in quitting drinking makes all the difference in achieving your goal of living an alcohol-free life. Rather than relying solely on willpower, think about making a toolkit that you will use to create a skill set for your sober journey.

You may have tried to quit drinking in the past. If so, identify what worked and what didn't work for you?

For example, do you need a community of like-minded people? Do you need a coach? Do you need more education? Do you need a plan to deal with triggers?

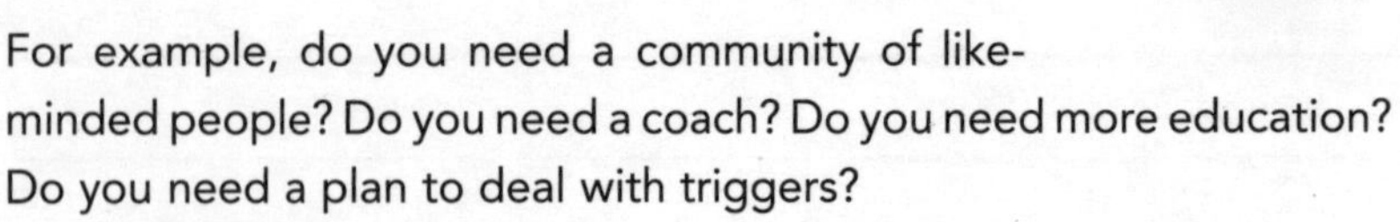

WHAT WORKED WELL | WHAT I NEED IN ADDITION

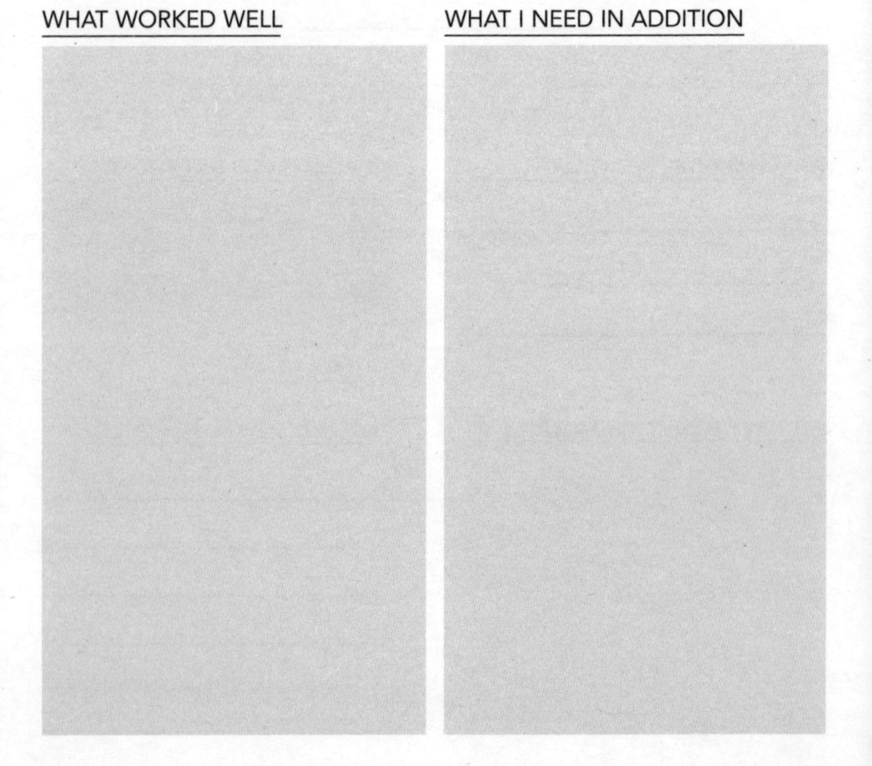

Date: __/__/__

HOW WOULD YOU RATE TODAY?

☆ ☆ ☆ ☆ ☆

WRITE ABOUT YOUR DAY

TOP 3 THINGS ABOUT TODAY

1.

2.

3.

HOW HAVE YOU FELT TODAY?

WHAT INSPIRED YOU THE MOST TODAY?

3 INTENTIONS FOR TOMORROW

1.

2.

3.

ACCOUNTABILITY

Accountability is about taking responsibility for your choices and actions through awareness and ownership.

5 ways to be accountable:

1. Find an accountability partner.
2. Share openly in a group.
3. Open up to close family or friends.
4. Get clear on what you stand to lose.
5. Be honest and authentic.

REFLECTIONS

FAMILY/FRIENDS YOU CAN COUNT ON

1.
2.
3.

GROUPS YOU COULD JOIN

PROSPECTIVE ACCOUNTABILITY PARTNERS:

1.
2.
3.

WHAT DO YOU STAND TO LOSE?

HOW YOU WILL DEMONSTRATE YOUR HONESTY OR AUTHENTICITY

1.
2.
3.
4.
5.

Date: __/__/__

HOW WOULD YOU RATE TODAY?

☆ ☆ ☆ ☆ ☆

WRITE ABOUT YOUR DAY

TOP 3 THINGS ABOUT TODAY

1.

2.

3.

HOW HAVE YOU FELT TODAY?

WHAT INSPIRED YOU THE MOST TODAY?

3 INTENTIONS FOR TOMORROW

1.

2.

3.

HOW TO QUESTION YOUR BELIEFS AND EMOTIONS

Get in the habit of writing in your journal about worries, fears or resentments interfering with your positive outlook. Analyse them on the basis of 5 questions:

1. Is it true?
2. How can I absolutely know it's true? (What actual evidence do you have to support the statement?)
3. How does the thought make me feel? (Use the emotion wheel on p. 80 for guidance.)
4. How does the thought make me behave?
5. Would I be a happier person without this thought?

Reflect on the fears or worries you might have about living an alcohol-free life. Use the 5 questions to examine one of your concerns.

ONE OF MY FEARS ABOUT LIVING AN AF LIFESTYLE IS:

1. Is it true?

2. How can I absolutely know it's true?

3. How does the thought make me feel?

4. How does the thought make me behave?

5. Would I be happier without the thought?

Date:__/__/__

HOW WOULD YOU RATE TODAY?

☆ ☆ ☆ ☆ ☆

WRITE ABOUT YOUR DAY

TOP 3 THINGS ABOUT TODAY

1.

2.

3.

HOW HAVE YOU FELT TODAY?

WHAT INSPIRED YOU THE MOST TODAY?

3 INTENTIONS FOR TOMORROW

1.

2.

3.

SHINING A LIGHT ON FALSE BELIEFS

Our beliefs can keep us stuck if we let them. By shining a light on any limiting beliefs you have about alcohol, you can see how they impact your life and whether they are benefiting or hindering you.

Begin to get clear on your beliefs by:

1. considering your behaviours
2. looking closer at your mindset.

Write down the beliefs that are holding you back from quitting alcohol.

1. List examples of how drinking has caused problems.
2. Look at the belief again to determine whether it's true. Think about using the 5 questions to examine your beliefs.
3. After you look at your beliefs, create statements using new, true beliefs.

EXAMPLE

BELIEF: Alcohol helps me relax.

Ways your drinking has caused problems:

I wake up with hangovers, argue with my partner and crave more alcohol.

Based on the evidence, is the belief true?

No, the alcohol relaxes me in the short term, but has the opposite effect soon after.

A more accurate, truthful statement would be:

I believe I might relax without alcohol in my life, and I want to find out if this really true.

Continued on next page

BELIEF:

Ways your drinking has caused problems:

Based on the evidence, is the belief true?

A more accurate, truthful statement would be:

BELIEF:

Ways your drinking has caused problems:

Based on the evidence, is the belief true?

A more accurate, truthful statement would be:

Date: ___/___/___

HOW WOULD YOU RATE TODAY?

☆ ☆ ☆ ☆ ☆

WRITE ABOUT YOUR DAY

TOP 3 THINGS ABOUT TODAY

1.

2.

3.

HOW HAVE YOU FELT TODAY?

WHAT INSPIRED YOU THE MOST TODAY?

3 INTENTIONS FOR TOMORROW

1.

2.

3.

YOU HAVE THE POWER

We have all been able to achieve goals in our life, especially when we have the right mindset and a strong reason why.

You already have the ability to achieve incredible things, especially when you are determined to make them happen. Think of the times in your life when you have set yourself a goal, been determined and made it happen.

TIMES I HAVE BEEN DETERMINED AND
HOW I ACHIEVED MY GOALS

Date: ___/___/___

HOW WOULD YOU RATE TODAY?

☆ ☆ ☆ ☆ ☆

WRITE ABOUT YOUR DAY

TOP 3 THINGS ABOUT TODAY

1.

2.

3.

HOW HAVE YOU FELT TODAY?

WHAT INSPIRED YOU THE MOST TODAY?

3 INTENTIONS FOR TOMORROW

1.

2.

3.

WHAT WON'T YOU COMPROMISE?

Drinkers often put alcohol ahead of the most important things in their lives and therefore compromise everything from relationships to careers and their health.

By becoming clear about what you are no longer prepared to put alcohol ahead of, you will feel empowered and motivated as you go forward.

WHAT HAVE YOU PUT ALCOHOL AHEAD OF?

WHAT IS MORE IMPORTANT TO YOU THAN ALCOHOL?

I AM NO LONGER WILLING TO PUT ALCOHOL AHEAD OF ...

Date: ___/___/___

HOW WOULD YOU RATE TODAY?

☆ ☆ ☆ ☆ ☆

WRITE ABOUT YOUR DAY

'Drunkenness is nothing but voluntary madness.'

—Seneca

TOP 3 THINGS ABOUT TODAY

1.

2.

3.

HOW HAVE YOU FELT TODAY?

WHAT INSPIRED YOU THE MOST TODAY?

3 INTENTIONS FOR TOMORROW

1.

2.

3.

YOUR LAST DRINK

What steps are you going to take to prepare for your last drink? Will you empty your house of alcohol? Will you announce it to family or friends? How will you spend your first evening alcohol-free? List all the possible ways you can prepare. When you take your last drink, write down what thoughts you have, how you feel, and what fears are going through your head.

Steps I will take before my last drink: ______________________

____

____

____

____

____

____

As I take my last drink, my thoughts and feelings include:

____

____

____

____

____

____

____

Date: __/__/__

HOW WOULD YOU RATE TODAY?

☆ ☆ ☆ ☆ ☆

WRITE ABOUT YOUR DAY

TOP 3 THINGS ABOUT TODAY

1.

2.

3.

HOW HAVE YOU FELT TODAY?

WHAT INSPIRED YOU THE MOST TODAY?

3 INTENTIONS FOR TOMORROW

1.

2.

3.

YOU CAN CHANGE YOUR HABITS

When you quit drinking, it's helpful to understand how alcohol factors into your daily life. Think about the drinking habits you have. Are you drinking every day? Or do you binge drink? At what time of day do you drink and what do you associate with that time? What shops do you frequent? Do you drink while cooking? Do you drink alone? Are you sneaking drinks when your spouse or partner isn't looking? Are you drinking at social gatherings? After work? In a pub or bar?

MY DRINKING HABITS

Date: __/__/__

HOW WOULD YOU RATE TODAY?

☆☆☆☆☆

WRITE ABOUT YOUR DAY

'We must despise all these temptations and pay no attention whatsoever to them.'

—Thérèse of Lisieux

TOP 3 THINGS ABOUT TODAY

1.

2.

3.

HOW HAVE YOU FELT TODAY?

WHAT INSPIRED YOU THE MOST TODAY?

3 INTENTIONS FOR TOMORROW

1.

2.

3.

YOUR SUBCONSCIOUS DEMON

Draw or describe your wine witch / beer gremlin / evil clown or other voice of your subconscious. When you feel tempted to drink, what thoughts go through your head?

Date: ___/___/___

HOW WOULD YOU RATE TODAY?

WRITE ABOUT YOUR DAY

'Goodbyes make you think. They make you realize what you've had, what you've lost, and what you've taken for granted.'

—Ritu Ghatourey

TOP 3 THINGS ABOUT TODAY

1.

2.

3.

HOW HAVE YOU FELT TODAY?

WHAT INSPIRED YOU THE MOST TODAY?

3 INTENTIONS FOR TOMORROW

1.

2.

3.

WRITE A FAREWELL LETTER TO ALCOHOL

When writing your farewell letter, include your reasons for quitting drinking, what you won't miss, and any regrets you have had about drinking.

Dear Alcohol,

Continued on next page

Date: __/__/__

HOW WOULD YOU RATE TODAY?

☆ ☆ ☆ ☆ ☆

WRITE ABOUT YOUR DAY

TOP 3 THINGS ABOUT TODAY

1.

2.

3.

HOW HAVE YOU FELT TODAY?

WHAT INSPIRED YOU THE MOST TODAY?

3 INTENTIONS FOR TOMORROW

1.

2.

3.

WORKING THROUGH CRAVINGS

Days 3–5 of the first week are the most challenging in the sober journey. It helps to have a strategy in place for shifting your mindset, whether that's doing star jumps, taking a walk, calling your accountability partner, or repeating a mantra to yourself.

What will be your strategy to shift your mindset from wanting to drink? What are some mantras you can say to yourself throughout the day to help create a positive attitude and enthusiasm for your new sober life? Famous quotes, meditative words and biblical verses are all examples of what others have found helpful. What kinds of self-care will you practise?

STRATEGIES	MANTRAS & QUOTES

Date: __/__/__

HOW WOULD YOU RATE TODAY?

☆ ☆ ☆ ☆ ☆

WRITE ABOUT YOUR DAY

TOP 3 THINGS ABOUT TODAY

1.

2.

3.

HOW HAVE YOU FELT TODAY?

WHAT INSPIRED YOU THE MOST TODAY?

3 INTENTIONS FOR TOMORROW

1.

2.

3.

IN CASE OF EMERGENCY

Write a letter to yourself that you can pull out and read if you feel overwhelming cravings to drink. Include all the reasons why you decided to be alcohol-free and describe how you would feel if you went back to drinking.

Explain to yourself why it is important to you to remain sober.

Dear me,

Continued on next page

Date: __/__/__

HOW WOULD YOU RATE TODAY?

☆ ☆ ☆ ☆ ☆

WRITE ABOUT YOUR DAY

TOP 3 THINGS ABOUT TODAY

1.

2.

3.

HOW HAVE YOU FELT TODAY?

WHAT INSPIRED YOU THE MOST TODAY?

3 INTENTIONS FOR TOMORROW

1.

2.

3.

UNCOMFORTABLE FEELINGS

Quitting drinking can cause uncomfortable feelings, especially in the early days of sobriety. What difficulties or challenges in life have you had to overcome in the past?

What strengths did you rely upon?

CHALLENGES I'VE FACED	STRENGTHS I RELIED UPON

Date: __/__/__

HOW WOULD YOU RATE TODAY?

☆ ☆ ☆ ☆ ☆

WRITE ABOUT YOUR DAY

TOP 3 THINGS ABOUT TODAY

1.

2.

3.

HOW HAVE YOU FELT TODAY?

WHAT INSPIRED YOU THE MOST TODAY?

3 INTENTIONS FOR TOMORROW

1.

2.

3.

LISTENING TO YOUR BODY

Beginning with today, pay attention to how your body is feeling by checking in regularly and noticing what is happening. Scan your body from head to toe and focus on any pain or, discomfort as well as the areas of your body that you like.

DATE: / /

HOW DOES YOUR BODY FEEL TODAY?

MARK WHERE YOU FEEL ANY PAIN

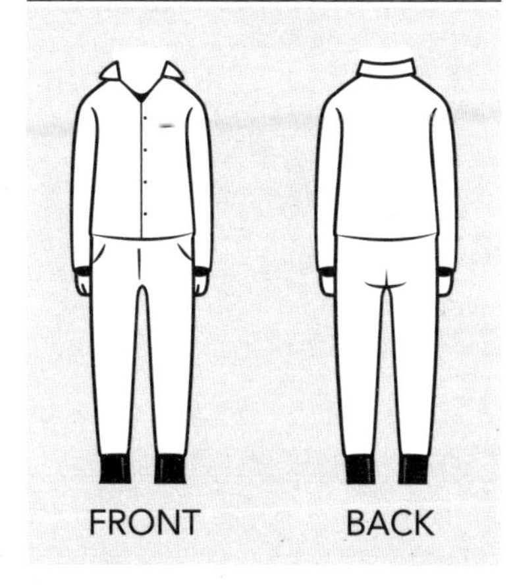

HOW DOES YOUR BODY MAKE YOU FEEL?

THINGS I LIKE ABOUT MY BODY

1.

2.

3.

4.

WHAT CAN YOU DO TO MAKE YOUR BODY HEALTHIER?

WHAT FOOD IS GOOD FOR YOUR BODY?

1.

2.

3.

HOW DOES YOUR BODY FEEL TODAY?

Date:__/__/__

HOW WOULD YOU RATE TODAY?

☆ ☆ ☆ ☆ ☆

WRITE ABOUT YOUR DAY

TOP 3 THINGS ABOUT TODAY

1.

2.

3.

HOW HAVE YOU FELT TODAY?

WHAT INSPIRED YOU THE MOST TODAY?

3 INTENTIONS FOR TOMORROW

1.

2.

3.

THE IMPACT ON HEALTH

Medical experts have linked alcohol to more than 60 types of disease or injury. What are some of the negative health consequences you have experienced from drinking? What are the top health concerns you have?

Negative health consequences include falling, blackouts, hangovers, high blood pressure, elevated liver enzymes, pre-diabetes, arthritis, bedwetting and many more conditions

General health concerns include diseases, cancer, chronic metabolic conditions such as diabetes, liver disease, heart failure, anxiety and depression, to name a few.

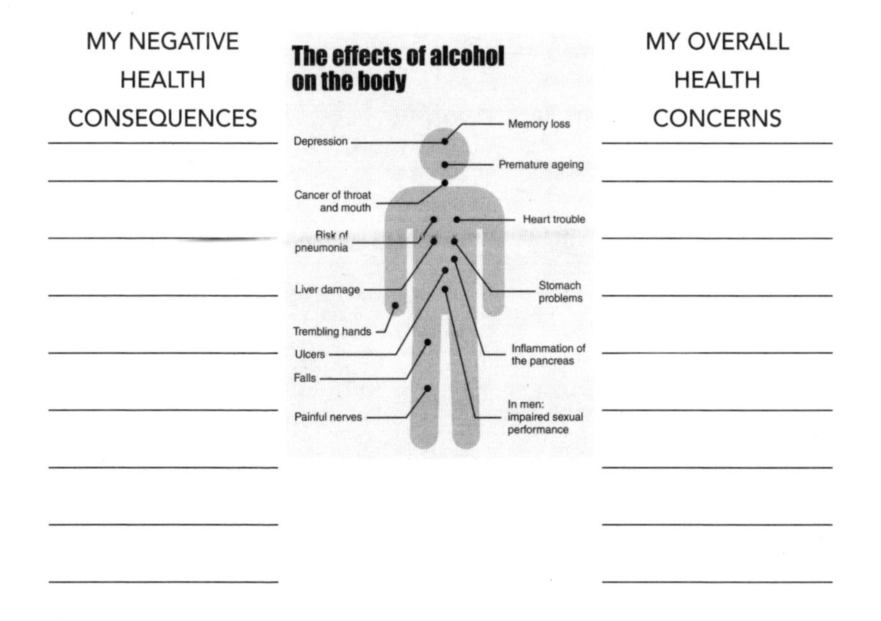

Consult your physician for any health concerns or consequences you may have or have had. Do not attempt to quit alcohol without seeking medical advice from your doctor.

Date:___/___/___

HOW WOULD YOU RATE TODAY?

☆ ☆ ☆ ☆ ☆

WRITE ABOUT YOUR DAY

TOP 3 THINGS ABOUT TODAY

1.

2.

3.

HOW HAVE YOU FELT TODAY?

WHAT INSPIRED YOU THE MOST TODAY?

3 INTENTIONS FOR TOMORROW

1.

2.

3.

REFLECTION

Alcohol impacts the brain in many ways:

Blackouts and memory loss, depression, anxiety, stress, anger, aggression, hangovers, mood changes, impaired thought processing, and sleep.

Review the list of health concerns you wrote down in the previous exercise. Write about your experiences with any or all of these effects. Be brutally honest with yourself.

Continued on next page

Date: __/__/__

HOW WOULD YOU RATE TODAY?

☆ ☆ ☆ ☆ ☆

WRITE ABOUT YOUR DAY

TOP 3 THINGS ABOUT TODAY

1.

2.

3.

HOW HAVE YOU FELT TODAY?

WHAT INSPIRED YOU THE MOST TODAY?

3 INTENTIONS FOR TOMORROW

1.

2.

3.

THE COST OF DRINKING ALCOHOL

When we drink, we do not always keep track of how much we are spending on alcohol, whether that's for home consumption, at restaurants, pubs or bars, for social occasions or on holidays. Try to calculate how much you spend in any given week, month and year on alcohol. What else could you be doing with that money?

WEEKLY COST

£/$__________

MONTHLY COST

£/$__________

YEARLY COST

£/$__________

WAYS I COULD BETTER USE THIS MONEY

Date: __/__/__

HOW WOULD YOU RATE TODAY?

☆ ☆ ☆ ☆ ☆

WRITE ABOUT YOUR DAY

'The rest of your life won't last forever.;

—Omar Khayyam

TOP 3 THINGS ABOUT TODAY

1.

2.

3.

HOW HAVE YOU FELT TODAY?

WHAT INSPIRED YOU THE MOST TODAY?

3 INTENTIONS FOR TOMORROW

1.

2.

3.

TIME CONSUMPTION

Do you wish you had more time?

Not only do we spend money on alcohol, we also spend a lot of *time* drinking – alone, with friends, at social gatherings, at sporting and entertainment events, on holidays and on flights. Estimate how much time you spend every day drinking. What activities or time with family or friends are you giving up? What are you missing out on?

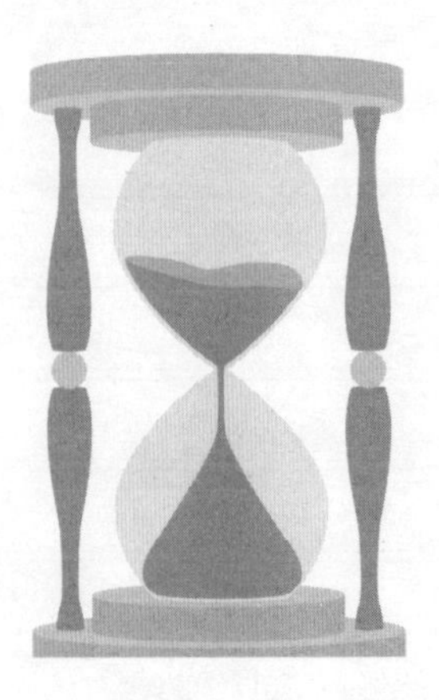

DAILY TIME SPENT DRINKING

[ ] hours

IF I WASN'T DRINKING, I COULD ...

- ○ ______________________________
- ○ ______________________________
- ○ ______________________________
- ○ ______________________________
- ○ ______________________________

Date: __/__/__

HOW WOULD YOU RATE TODAY?

☆ ☆ ☆ ☆ ☆

WRITE ABOUT YOUR DAY

TOP 3 THINGS ABOUT TODAY

1.

2.

3.

HOW HAVE YOU FELT TODAY?

WHAT INSPIRED YOU THE MOST TODAY?

3 INTENTIONS FOR TOMORROW

1.

2.

3.

ALTERNATIVES TO ALCOHOL

Make a list of non-alcoholic drinks you have found enjoyable and could use them as your 'go to' when relaxing at home or attending a social gathering. What other ways can you keep your hands or mind occupied to replace the activity of drinking?

BEVERAGES I ENJOY	WAYS TO OCCUPY MY HANDS

Date: ___/___/___

HOW WOULD YOU RATE TODAY?

☆ ☆ ☆ ☆ ☆

WRITE ABOUT YOUR DAY

TOP 3 THINGS ABOUT TODAY

1.

2.

3.

HOW HAVE YOU FELT TODAY?

WHAT INSPIRED YOU THE MOST TODAY?

3 INTENTIONS FOR TOMORROW

1.

2.

3.

WHO YOU REALLY ARE

If you have been struggling with alcohol, remind yourself that this is not who you are, but it is simply where you are at this point in time.

Use the space below to get clear on who you really are.

Try and come up with as many statements as you can. For example: 'Without alcohol I will be a better parent who listens more and feels connected to my kids.'

Without alcohol I will be ...

Date: __/__/__

HOW WOULD YOU RATE TODAY?

☆ ☆ ☆ ☆ ☆

WRITE ABOUT YOUR DAY

'Once you label me you negate me.'

—Søren Kierkegaard

TOP 3 THINGS ABOUT TODAY

1.

2.

3.

HOW HAVE YOU FELT TODAY?

WHAT INSPIRED YOU THE MOST TODAY?

3 INTENTIONS FOR TOMORROW

1.

2.

3.

DESCRIBING YOUR NEW ALCOHOL-FREE LIFESTYLE

When you decide to live an alcohol-free life, it can be difficult to describe yourself to others. Think about where you are now on your journey as compared to where you were when you quit drinking. What word or words describe how you see yourself on the spectrum of alcohol use (e.g. grey area drinker, high-functioning drinker, heavy drinker, habitual drinker)?

What word or words would best describe how you see yourself in the alcohol-free world (e.g., sober, sober-rebel, non-drinker, ex-drinker, teetotal)?

WORDS THAT DESCRIBE MYSELF ON THE SPECTRUM OF ALCOHOL USE

WORDS THAT DESCRIBE HOW I SEE MYSELF IN THE ALCOHOL-FREE WORLD

Date: __/__/__

HOW WOULD YOU RATE TODAY?

☆ ☆ ☆ ☆ ☆

WRITE ABOUT YOUR DAY

TOP 3 THINGS ABOUT TODAY

1.

2.

3.

HOW HAVE YOU FELT TODAY?

WHAT INSPIRED YOU THE MOST TODAY?

3 INTENTIONS FOR TOMORROW

1.

2.

3.

MOTIVATION

Staying motivated and excited is vital to success in your sober journey. Take time to identify what motivates you to succeed. Identify what gives you joy. What are some of the dreams and aspirations you have for your new sober life?

I AM MOTIVATED BY ...

I FIND JOY IN ...

3 OF MY DREAMS AND ASPIRATIONS ARE ...

1.

2.

3.

Date: ___/___/___

HOW WOULD YOU RATE TODAY?

☆ ☆ ☆ ☆ ☆

WRITE ABOUT YOUR DAY

TOP 3 THINGS ABOUT TODAY

1.

2.

3.

HOW HAVE YOU FELT TODAY?

WHAT INSPIRED YOU THE MOST TODAY?

3 INTENTIONS FOR TOMORROW

1.

2.

3.

FREEDOM PLAN

Outline a short freedom plan for yourself. Include priorities, values, long- and short-term goals, hopes and dreams. What do you need to do to achieve success in your freedom plan?

MY PRIORITIES IN LIFE

1.
2.
3.

MY LONG-TERM GOALS

1.
2.
3.

MY HOPES AND DREAMS

1.
2.
3.

MY SHORT-TERM GOALS

1.
2.
3.

WHAT I NEED TO DO TO ACHIEVE MY FREEDOM PLAN

Date: __/__/__

HOW WOULD YOU RATE TODAY?

☆ ☆ ☆ ☆ ☆

WRITE ABOUT YOUR DAY

TOP 3 THINGS ABOUT TODAY

1.

2.

3.

HOW HAVE YOU FELT TODAY?

WHAT INSPIRED YOU THE MOST TODAY?

3 INTENTIONS FOR TOMORROW

1.

2.

3.

PLEDGE TO MYSELF

Write a pledge to yourself affirming your priorities. Write a new belief statement about a sober lifestyle.

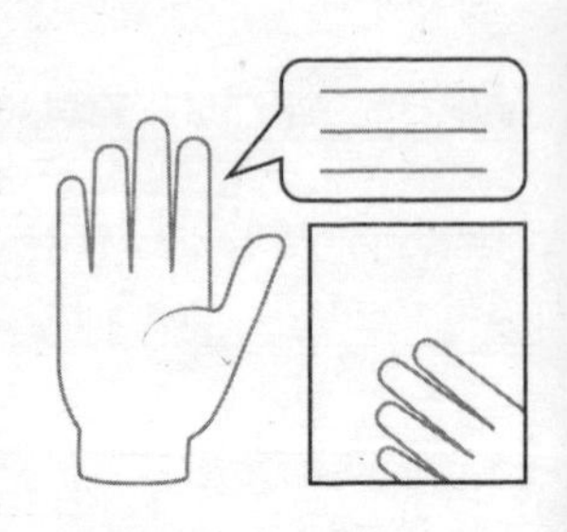

EXAMPLE

I believe that my life and health ... I believe that I am ... I believe that I can do ... I am willing to do ___ for myself to be a lifelong non-drinker.

I believe ____

____

____

____

____

____

____

____

____

____

____

____

____

Date: __/__/__

HOW WOULD YOU RATE TODAY?

☆ ☆ ☆ ☆ ☆

WRITE ABOUT YOUR DAY

TOP 3 THINGS ABOUT TODAY

1.

2.

3.

HOW HAVE YOU FELT TODAY?

WHAT INSPIRED YOU THE MOST TODAY?

3 INTENTIONS FOR TOMORROW

1.

2.

3.

SWOT ANALYSIS

Businesses conduct a SWOT analysis to get clear about potential risks and opportunities in order that they can take positive action. You can use the same method in sobriety to set yourself up for success and avoid any potential pitfalls.

Create your analysis by getting clear on:
1. your **S**trengths; 2. your **W**eaknesses; 3. **O**pportunities that being sober will create; and 4. **T**hreats (people, places, behaviours).

YOUR STRENGTHS IN SOBRIETY

YOUR WEAKNESSES IN SOBRIETY

YOUR OPPORTUNITIES

THREATS TO YOUR SOBRIETY

Date: __/__/__

HOW WOULD YOU RATE TODAY?

☆ ☆ ☆ ☆ ☆

WRITE ABOUT YOUR DAY

TOP 3 THINGS ABOUT TODAY

1.

2.

3.

HOW HAVE YOU FELT TODAY?

WHAT INSPIRED YOU THE MOST TODAY?

3 INTENTIONS FOR TOMORROW

1.

2.

3.

PLANNING FOR LONG-TERM SOBRIETY

Review the threats to your sobriety, your habits list and your beliefs about alcohol. Make a more complete list of threats by thinking of everything that could potentially pose a threat to your remaining alcohol free and explain why. Think about people, places, thoughts, things you associate with alcohol such as parties, habits, difficult situations and so on. Next to each threat, write your plan to prevent a slip back to drinking.

Threat: ____________________

Plan to prevent a slip: ____________________

____

____

Threat: ____________________

Plan to prevent a slip: ____________________

____

____

Threat: ____________________

Plan to prevent a slip: ____________________

____

____

Continued on next page

Threat: ____________________

Plan to prevent a slip: ____________________

____

____

Threat: ____________________

Plan to prevent a slip: ____________________

____

____

Threat: ____________________

Plan to prevent a slip: ____________________

____

____

Threat: ____________________

Plan to prevent a slip: ____________________

____

____

Threat: ____________________

Plan to prevent a slip: ____________________

____

____

Continued on next page

Threat: ______________________________

Plan to prevent a slip: ______________________________

____

____

Threat: ______________________________

Plan to prevent a slip: ______________________________

____

____

Threat: ______________________________

Plan to prevent a slip: ______________________________

____

____

Threat: ______________________________

Plan to prevent a slip: ______________________________

____

____

Threat: ______________________________

Plan to prevent a slip: ______________________________

____

____

Date: __/__/__

HOW WOULD YOU RATE TODAY?

☆ ☆ ☆ ☆ ☆

WRITE ABOUT YOUR DAY

TOP 3 THINGS ABOUT TODAY

1.

2.

3.

HOW HAVE YOU FELT TODAY?

WHAT INSPIRED YOU THE MOST TODAY?

3 INTENTIONS FOR TOMORROW

1.

2.

3.

REFLECTION

During the first 6 weeks of quitting drinking, emotions can run raw and anxiety can surge as the brain begins to recalibrate. What types of difficult emotions have you encountered? Are you repressing those moods or finding ways to cope with them? Reflect on the ways you have discovered to release your negative feelings, as well as how you find yourself coping in difficult situations. What progress do you see? Are there areas for improvement? How might you better deal with emotional strains?

Continued on next page

Date: __/__/__

HOW WOULD YOU RATE TODAY?

☆ ☆ ☆ ☆ ☆

WRITE ABOUT YOUR DAY

TOP 3 THINGS ABOUT TODAY

1.

2.

3.

HOW HAVE YOU FELT TODAY?

WHAT INSPIRED YOU THE MOST TODAY?

3 INTENTIONS FOR TOMORROW

1.

2.

3.

YOUR CORE VALUES

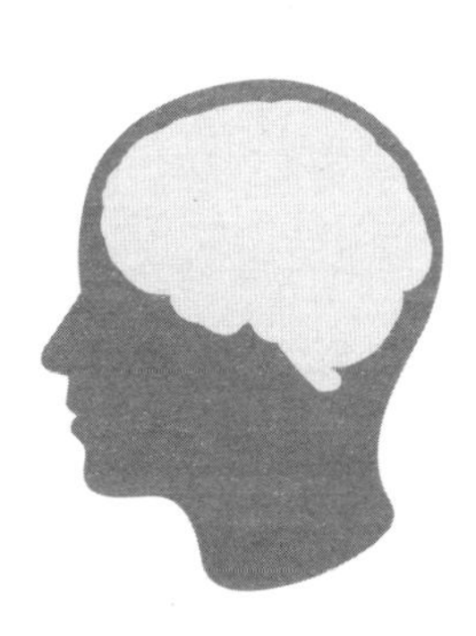

Understanding your values will help you know yourself better so you can do more of what you love and less of the things that cause you emotional suffering.

Below, in the left-hand column, is a checklist of core values. Without overthinking, circle 6–8 values from the list that you feel are important to you and describe you best.

In the right-hand column make a list of the 6–8 qualities on the list that you admire most in others.

On the next page, identify where in your life you have exhibited the qualities you consider your priorities.

VALUES CHECKLIST

MY TOP VALUES		VALUES I ADMIRE IN OTHERS
Achievement	Leadership	1
Authenticity	Learning	
Autonomy	Love	
Balance	Loyalty	2
Beauty	Meaningful work	
Challenge	Openness	
Community	Optimism	3
Compassion	Peace	
Competency	Pleasure	
Creativity	Reputation	4
Curiosity	Respect	
Fairness	Responsibility	
Faith	Security	5
Fame	Self-respect	
Fun	Service	
Growth	Spirituality	6
Happiness	Stability	
Honesty	Success	7
Humour	Trustworthiness	
Justice	Wealth	
Kindness	Wisdom	8
Knowledge		

Continued on next page

VALUE	WHERE I HAVE EXHIBITED MY CORE VALUES
1.	
2.	
3.	
4.	
5.	
6.	
7.	
8.	

Date: __/__/__

HOW WOULD YOU RATE TODAY?

☆ ☆ ☆ ☆ ☆

WRITE ABOUT YOUR DAY

TOP 3 THINGS ABOUT TODAY

1.

2.

3.

HOW HAVE YOU FELT TODAY?

WHAT INSPIRED YOU THE MOST TODAY?

3 INTENTIONS FOR TOMORROW

1.

2.

3.

PEOPLE, PLACES AND THINGS THAT ADD VALUE TO MY LIFE

When we live our life in line with our core values, we minimize emotional discomfort.

Use the exercise below to gain clarity about how you can make changes to honour your values and invite more peace, calm and happiness into your life. Referring to your list of values, add people, places and things into the boxes below according to whether they are aligned or not aligned with these values.

ALIGNED WITH MY VALUES	NOT ALIGNED WITH MY VALUES

Date: __/__/__

HOW WOULD YOU RATE TODAY?

☆ ☆ ☆ ☆ ☆

WRITE ABOUT YOUR DAY

TOP 3 THINGS ABOUT TODAY

1.

2.

3.

HOW HAVE YOU FELT TODAY?

WHAT INSPIRED YOU THE MOST TODAY?

3 INTENTIONS FOR TOMORROW

1.

2.

3.

MY MOST IMPORTANT AREAS IN LIFE

Consider all the areas of your life and how satisfied with them you currently are and how important they are to you. What might you need to change in order to see improvement?

Complete the next four pages.

WORK & CAREER

HEALTH & WELLNESS

MONEY & FINANCES

Continued on next page

FAMILY

RELATIONSHIPS WITH OTHERS

INTIMATE RELATIONSHIPS

SELF-CARE

Continued on next page

RELIGION & SPIRITUALITY

PERSONAL GROWTH & EDUCATION

CAREGIVING & HELPING OTHERS

COMMUNITY INVOLVEMENT

Continued on next page

LEISURE ACTIVITIES & HOBBIES

OTHER

OTHER

OTHER

Date: __/__/__

HOW WOULD YOU RATE TODAY?

☆ ☆ ☆ ☆ ☆

WRITE ABOUT YOUR DAY

TOP 3 THINGS ABOUT TODAY

1.

2.

3.

HOW HAVE YOU FELT TODAY?

WHAT INSPIRED YOU THE MOST TODAY?

3 INTENTIONS FOR TOMORROW

1.

2.

3.

REFLECTION

Reflect on the concept of being authentic.

Are there people/places/situations that cause you to struggle and/or mask who you are and what you really feel? What could you change in order to be less affected by these influences?

Continued on next page

Date: __/__/__

HOW WOULD YOU RATE TODAY?

☆ ☆ ☆ ☆ ☆

WRITE ABOUT YOUR DAY

TOP 3 THINGS ABOUT TODAY

1.

2.

3.

HOW HAVE YOU FELT TODAY?

WHAT INSPIRED YOU THE MOST TODAY?

3 INTENTIONS FOR TOMORROW

1.

2.

3.

HOW ARE YOU FEELING?

Use the emotion wheel to bring awareness to how you are feeling right now.

NORMAL

- Fearful
  - Scared: Helpless, Frightened
  - Anxious: Overwhelmed, Worried
  - Insecure: Inadequate, Inferior
  - Weak: Worthless, Insignificant
  - Rejected: Excluded, Persecuted
  - Threatened: Nervous, Exposed
- Angry
  - Let down: Betrayed, Resentful
  - Humiliated: Disrespected, Ridiculed
  - Bitter: Indignant, Violated
  - Mad: Furious, Jealous
  - Aggressive: Provoked, Hostile
  - Frustrated: Infuriated, Annoyed
  - Distant: Withdrawn, Numb
  - Critical: Sceptical, Dismissive
- Disgusted
  - Disapproving: Judgmental, Embarrassed
  - Disappointed: Appalled, Revolted
  - Awful: Nauseated, Detestable
  - Repelled: Horrified, Hesitant
- Sad
  - Hurt: Embarrassed, Disappointed
  - Depressed: Inferior, Empty
  - Guilty: Remorseful, Ashamed
  - Despair: Powerless, Grief
  - Vulnerable: Fragile, Victimised
  - Lonely: Abandoned, Isolated
- Happy
  - Optimistic: Inspired, Hopeful
  - Trusting: Intimate, Sensitive
  - Peaceful: Thankful, Loving
  - Powerful: Creative, Courageous
  - Accepted: Valued, Respected
  - Proud: Confident, Successful
  - Interested: Inquisitive, Curious
  - Content: Joyful, Free
  - Playful: Cheeky, Aroused
- Surprised
  - Excited: Energetic, Eager
  - Amazed: Awe, Astonished
  - Confused: Perplexed, Disillusioned
  - Startled: Dismayed, Shocked
- Bad
  - Tired: Unfocussed, Sleepy
  - Stressed: Out of control, Overwhelmed
  - Busy: Rushed, Pressured
  - Bored: Apathetic, Indifferent

Date: __/__/__

HOW WOULD YOU RATE TODAY?

☆ ☆ ☆ ☆ ☆

WRITE ABOUT YOUR DAY

TOP 3 THINGS ABOUT TODAY

1.

2.

3.

HOW HAVE YOU FELT TODAY?

WHAT INSPIRED YOU THE MOST TODAY?

3 INTENTIONS FOR TOMORROW

1.

2.

3.

PIES CHECK-IN PROCESS

A great way to get clear on how you are really feeling is to use the PIES check-in process to look closer at each area of your wellbeing.

Use the space below to explore how you currently feel – **P**hysically, **I**ntellectually **E**motionally and **S**piritually.

You can build a deeper connection with a partner or loved one by sharing your check-in with each other.

PHYSICALLY I AM FEELING ...

INTELLECTUALLY I AM FEELING ...

EMOTIONALLY I AM FEELING ...

SPIRITUALLY I AM FEELING ...

Date: __/__/__

HOW WOULD YOU RATE TODAY?

☆ ☆ ☆ ☆ ☆

WRITE ABOUT YOUR DAY

TOP 3 THINGS ABOUT TODAY

1.

2.

3.

HOW HAVE YOU FELT TODAY?

WHAT INSPIRED YOU THE MOST TODAY?

3 INTENTIONS FOR TOMORROW

1.

2.

3.

EMOTIONS DETERMINE OUR ACTIONS

Write down three occasions when you have reacted irrationally or childishly.

After you review your statements, using the emotion wheel on p. 80, identify what it was you were feeling on those occasions. What did you need for emotional support?

As you review the behaviour in contrast with what you needed, are you able to see a link to past childhood trauma or neglect from parents, teachers, siblings or other family members or friends?

TIMES I REACTED IRRATIONALLY OR CHILDISHLY & MY EMOTION	SIMILARITY TO MY PAST OR CHILDHOOD
1.	1.
2.	2.
3.	3.

Date: __/__/__

HOW WOULD YOU RATE TODAY?

☆ ☆ ☆ ☆ ☆

WRITE ABOUT YOUR DAY

'Do not lose hold of your dreams or aspirations, for if you do, you may still exist, but you have ceased to live.'
– Henry David Thoreau

TOP 3 THINGS ABOUT TODAY

1.

2.

3.

HOW HAVE YOU FELT TODAY?

WHAT INSPIRED YOU THE MOST TODAY?

3 INTENTIONS FOR TOMORROW

1.

2.

3.

REFLECTION

Write about your goals and aspirations.

Review your freedom plan (p. 54) and SWOT analysis (p. 58). What obstacles do you need to overcome to achieve those goals and what will be your plan of action? How will your emotions factor into your plan of action?

Continued on next page

Date: __/__/__

HOW WOULD YOU RATE TODAY?

WRITE ABOUT YOUR DAY

TOP 3 THINGS ABOUT TODAY

1.

2.

3.

HOW HAVE YOU FELT TODAY?

WHAT INSPIRED YOU THE MOST TODAY?

3 INTENTIONS FOR TOMORROW

1.

2.

3.

YOUR CHRONOLOGY

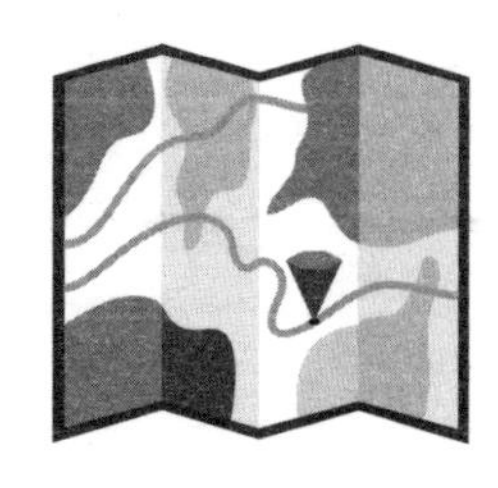

Draw or outline a timeline of your life. What emotions do you associate with happy points in time and painful points in time? Are there other emotions you frequently have that can be traced to an event/person/situation in your life? Are there any associations with alcohol during these events?

Date: ___/___/___

HOW WOULD YOU RATE TODAY?

☆ ☆ ☆ ☆ ☆

WRITE ABOUT YOUR DAY

'What lies behind us and what lies before us are tiny matters compared to what lies within us.'

—Ralph Waldo Emerson

TOP 3 THINGS ABOUT TODAY

1.

2.

3.

HOW HAVE YOU FELT TODAY?

WHAT INSPIRED YOU THE MOST TODAY?

3 INTENTIONS FOR TOMORROW

1.

2.

3.

REFLECTION: COGNITIVE DISSONANCE & SOBRIETY

As you reflect on your personal timeline (p. 89), describe the point where your mindset shifted to cognitive dissonance – that is, when you realized your drinking was out of control and you wanted to give up drinking but felt at war with yourself. If you had setbacks in the past, what have you learned about what you may have needed to avoid those lapses? What other realizations about sobriety have you considered?

Continued on next page

Date: __/__/__

HOW WOULD YOU RATE TODAY?

☆ ☆ ☆ ☆ ☆

WRITE ABOUT YOUR DAY

TOP 3 THINGS ABOUT TODAY

1.

2.

3.

HOW HAVE YOU FELT TODAY?

WHAT INSPIRED YOU THE MOST TODAY?

3 INTENTIONS FOR TOMORROW

1.

2.

3.

YOUR NEW ALCOHOL-FREE LIFE

One of the ways to stay motivated to quit drinking is to remain excited about your new lifestyle. What excites you about living an alcohol-free life? What are the joys in life that you have or hope to have by quitting drinking?

WHAT I'M EXCITED ABOUT	JOYS IN LIFE I HAVE DISCOVERED

Date: ___/___/___

HOW WOULD YOU RATE TODAY?

☆ ☆ ☆ ☆ ☆

WRITE ABOUT YOUR DAY

TOP 3 THINGS ABOUT TODAY

1.

2.

3.

HOW HAVE YOU FELT TODAY?

WHAT INSPIRED YOU THE MOST TODAY?

3 INTENTIONS FOR TOMORROW

1.

2.

3.

LIFE WITHOUT ALCOHOL

Write about areas in your life that you think will be less fun without alcohol and write a challenge statement for each one of those examples.

EXAMPLE

Belief: I don't think weddings will be as much fun without alcohol.

Challenge statement: But when I am at a wedding and drunk, I embarrass myself and then I can't remember what I said or did that got my partner/spouse so angry.

Belief:

Challenge statement:

Belief:

Challenge statement:

Belief:

Challenge statement:

Date: __/__/__

HOW WOULD YOU RATE TODAY?

☆ ☆ ☆ ☆ ☆

WRITE ABOUT YOUR DAY

TOP 3 THINGS ABOUT TODAY

1.

2.

3.

HOW HAVE YOU FELT TODAY?

WHAT INSPIRED YOU THE MOST TODAY?

3 INTENTIONS FOR TOMORROW

1.

2.

3.

REFLECTION

As you examine aspects of your self-awareness, what insights about your values, emotions, motivations and commitment have you discovered? What fears or concerns remain about an alcohol-free life?

Continued on next page

Date:__/__/__

HOW WOULD YOU RATE TODAY?

☆ ☆ ☆ ☆ ☆

WRITE ABOUT YOUR DAY

'The only difference between a rut and a grave are the dimensions.'

—Ellen Glasgow

TOP 3 THINGS ABOUT TODAY

1.

2.

3.

HOW HAVE YOU FELT TODAY?

WHAT INSPIRED YOU THE MOST TODAY?

3 INTENTIONS FOR TOMORROW

1.

2.

3.

NEGATIVE THOUGHTS

Write down some examples of how you have been critical of yourself or become negative about yourself. Using those statements, write down what you would say to your best friend if they approached you for support in the same circumstances. Do any of these negative statements link to childhood trauma or experiences with parents, family, teachers or friends?

Negative thought:

Your response to a friend:

Is the thought linked to a trauma or experience?

A more accurate, truthful statement would be:

Negative thought:

Your response to a friend:

Is the thought linked to a trauma or experience?

A more accurate, truthful statement would be:

Continued on next page

Negative thought:

Your response to a friend:

Is the thought linked to a trauma or experience?

A more accurate, truthful statement would be:

Negative thought:

Your response to a friend:

Is the thought linked to a trauma or experience?

A more accurate, truthful statement would be:

Negative thought:

Your response to a friend:

Is the thought linked to a trauma or experience?

A more accurate, truthful statement would be:

Date: __/__/__

HOW WOULD YOU RATE TODAY?

☆ ☆ ☆ ☆ ☆

WRITE ABOUT YOUR DAY

TOP 3 THINGS ABOUT TODAY

1.

2.

3.

HOW HAVE YOU FELT TODAY?

WHAT INSPIRED YOU THE MOST TODAY?

3 INTENTIONS FOR TOMORROW

1.

2.

3.

NEGATIVE TRAITS ANALYSIS

Overthinking, worrying and anxiety are common among people who develop addictions. These behaviours often stem from childhood or past experiences. Begin to notice what triggers you and draw parallels with the way you were treated by your mother or father, siblings or others in your life. Start by examining your own negative traits and then link them to a person, place or situation.

On the next two pages, create a negative traits analysis for yourself. Include the following information:

1. Your negative trait
2. Person to whom you attribute this trait (parent, sibling, teacher, friend) and why
3. Whether your friends contribute to your negative behaviour or just the people you don't like.

EXAMPLE

Negative trait: Unable to take criticism

How I see this trait: I see criticism as rejection due to my fear of abandonment.

Person with whom I attribute this trait: I believe my mum also struggles with this. When I have made any constructive criticism in the past, she has become upset. Yet she often criticizes me and rarely acknowledges my achievements in life.

People I like: do not criticize me.

People I dislike: have criticized me at some point. This includes work colleagues, family members and friends and always leads to conflict.

Continued on next page

Negative trait:

How I see this trait:

Person with whom I attribute this trait and why:

People I like:

People I dislike:

Negative trait:

How I see this trait:

Person with whom I attribute this trait and why:

People I like:

People I dislike:

Negative trait:

How I see this trait:

Person with whom I attribute this trait and why:

People I like:

People I dislike:

Negative trait:

How I see this trait:

Person with whom I attribute this trait and why:

People I like:

People I dislike:

Date: __/__/__

HOW WOULD YOU RATE TODAY?

☆ ☆ ☆ ☆ ☆

WRITE ABOUT YOUR DAY

TOP 3 THINGS ABOUT TODAY

1.

2.

3.

HOW HAVE YOU FELT TODAY?

WHAT INSPIRED YOU THE MOST TODAY?

3 INTENTIONS FOR TOMORROW

1.

2.

3.

REWARDING YOURSELF

When we quit drinking, our neurological pathways recalibrate to find a more balanced level of dopamine and serotonin. These are the 'feel good' chemicals released when we experience pleasure. After quitting drinking, it may take some time to experience natural levels of dopamine and serotonin.

What are some daily natural rewards that you can incorporate into your day to help your brain rebalance its pleasure signals? Physical rewards could be long walks, bicycle rides, dancing or hobbies. Spiritual rewards could be music, art or meditation.

PHYSICAL REWARDS	SPIRITUAL REWARDS

Date: __/__/__

HOW WOULD YOU RATE TODAY?

WRITE ABOUT YOUR DAY

TOP 3 THINGS ABOUT TODAY

1.

2.

3.

HOW HAVE YOU FELT TODAY?

WHAT INSPIRED YOU THE MOST TODAY?

3 INTENTIONS FOR TOMORROW

1.

2.

3.

CELEBRATING MILESTONES

Celebrating your sober milestones is an effective way to stay motivated and excited throughout your first year alcohol-free. Many people find that they continue to be excited about their new lives if they have something to work towards.

What will be significant milestones for you as you venture on your sober journey? How will you celebrate and/or reward your successes?

30 DAYS

____

60 DAYS

____

90 DAYS

____

100 DAYS

____

365 DAYS – SOBERVESARY!

____

Date: __/__/__

HOW WOULD YOU RATE TODAY?

☆ ☆ ☆ ☆ ☆

WRITE ABOUT YOUR DAY

'Arriving at one goal is the starting point to another.'

–John Dewey

TOP 3 THINGS ABOUT TODAY

1.

2.

3.

HOW HAVE YOU FELT TODAY?

WHAT INSPIRED YOU THE MOST TODAY?

3 INTENTIONS FOR TOMORROW

1.

2.

3.

MILESTONE GOALS

In addition to planning celebrations for your milestones, it is also important to set goals for each of them. Goals might include adding exercise, improving nutrition, continued study and learning about the effects of alcohol, or other aspirations such as blogging, mentoring or career changes.

GOALS:

1. ....
2. ....
3. ....
4. ....
5. ....

Review your milestones and add goals for each one.

MY GOALS FOR 30 DAYS

MY GOALS FOR 60 DAYS

Continued on next page

MY GOALS FOR 30 DAYS

MY GOALS FOR 60 DAYS

MY GOALS FOR 365 DAYS – SOBERVERSARY!

Date: __/__/__

HOW WOULD YOU RATE TODAY?

☆ ☆ ☆ ☆ ☆

WRITE ABOUT YOUR DAY

TOP 3 THINGS ABOUT TODAY

1.

2.

3.

HOW HAVE YOU FELT TODAY?

WHAT INSPIRED YOU THE MOST TODAY?

3 INTENTIONS FOR TOMORROW

1.

2.

3.

ONGOING SELF-CARE

Small steps every day

Finding balance in everyday life is critical to ongoing freedom from alcohol. Review your list on p. 108 where you identified physical and spiritual rewards. In addition to those activities, you may find other types of support helpful to continue self growth and education, such as meditation, yoga, religion, therapy, social media support groups, reading, taking a course, nutrition and physical exercise.

What acts of self-care will help you develop ongoing self-acceptance and awareness?

Date: ___/___/___

HOW WOULD YOU RATE TODAY?

☆ ☆ ☆ ☆ ☆

WRITE ABOUT YOUR DAY

TOP 3 THINGS ABOUT TODAY

1.

2.

3.

HOW HAVE YOU FELT TODAY?

WHAT INSPIRED YOU THE MOST TODAY?

3 INTENTIONS FOR TOMORROW

1.

2.

3.

DREAM JOURNAL

Our dreams act like a gateway into our subconscious mind, and when we quit drinking it is common to experience powerful and vivid dreams.

Use the space below to make a note of any dreams you experience so you can explore them further. You might find it helpful to create a separate dream journal.

Date: ___/___/___

HOW WOULD YOU RATE TODAY?

☆ ☆ ☆ ☆ ☆

WRITE ABOUT YOUR DAY

TOP 3 THINGS ABOUT TODAY

1.

2.

3.

HOW HAVE YOU FELT TODAY?

WHAT INSPIRED YOU THE MOST TODAY?

3 INTENTIONS FOR TOMORROW

1.

2.

3.

REFLECTION

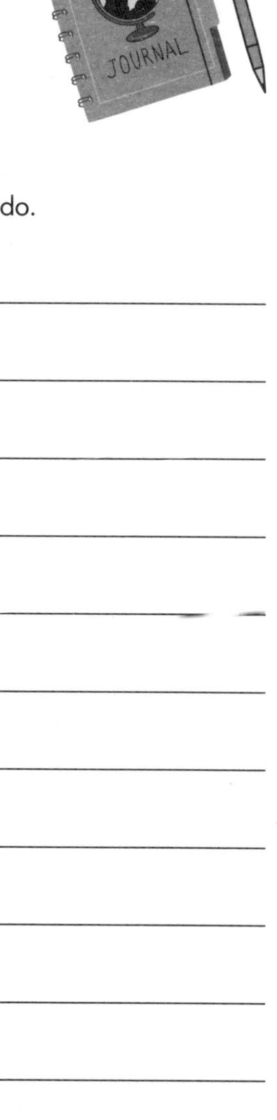

Review your journal pages on negative thoughts (p. 101) and traits (p. 104), as well as your plans for ongoing self-care (p. 115), rewards (p. 108) and milestones (pp. 110). In what ways is sobriety becoming easier? What are some examples of positive changes you are experiencing? Are you having ongoing challenges remaining alcohol-free? Identify them and reflect on what additional work you might still need to do.

Continued on next page

Date:__/__/__

HOW WOULD YOU RATE TODAY?

☆ ☆ ☆ ☆ ☆

WRITE ABOUT YOUR DAY

TOP 3 THINGS ABOUT TODAY

1.

2.

3.

HOW HAVE YOU FELT TODAY?

WHAT INSPIRED YOU THE MOST TODAY?

3 INTENTIONS FOR TOMORROW

1.

2.

3.

COMING OUT

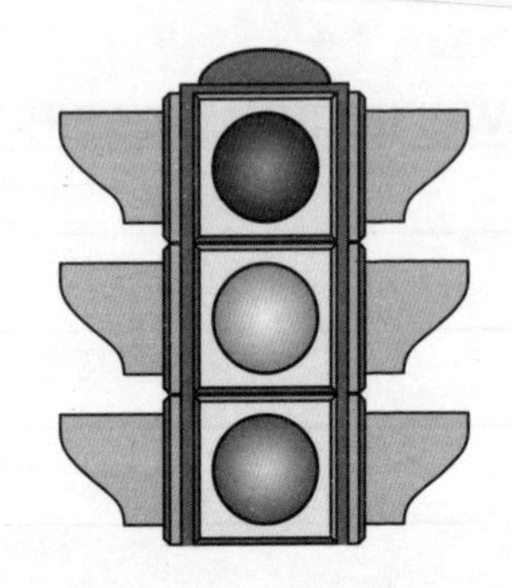

It can be a dilemma whether or not to share with your family or friends that you no longer drink. Sometimes, it can create awkward situations, particularly when others are not comfortable around non-drinkers.

Using the analogy of a stoplight, identify the people whom you consider to be red light (those uncomfortable knowing about your freedom from alcohol), amber light (people with whom you need to exercise caution) and green light (those with whom you are free to discuss anything).

RED LIGHT PEOPLE

AMBER LIGHT PEOPLE

GREEN LIGHT PEOPLE

TALKING POINTS FOR COMING OUT

Date: __/__/__

HOW WOULD YOU RATE TODAY?

☆ ☆ ☆ ☆ ☆

WRITE ABOUT YOUR DAY

'Memory is the diary that we all carry about with us.'

—Oscar Wilde

TOP 3 THINGS ABOUT TODAY

1.

2.

3.

HOW HAVE YOU FELT TODAY?

WHAT INSPIRED YOU THE MOST TODAY?

3 INTENTIONS FOR TOMORROW

1.

2.

3.

FADING AFFECT BIAS – FAB

Fading affect bias (FAB) is a term psychologists use to describe the phenomenon of positive memories outlasting the negative memories of an experience. When we quit drinking, the brain quickly removes negative associations so that the emotional pain heals and is replaced by positive associations. FAB can catch you off guard with no warning. When that happens, you will need to cope with those thoughts and dispel any cravings that might occur.

Write down how you will smash any remaining false beliefs you may have about alcohol. What do you need in terms of support, education, accountability and coaching? What books have you found helpful to better understand the effects of alcohol?

When I experience FAB, I will:____________________

Continued on next page

Beliefs about alcohol that I need to continue to address:

Strategies I have found helpful in countering my false beliefs:

Books I have found helpful or plan to read:

Additional thoughts I have about FAB:

Date: ___/___/___

HOW WOULD YOU RATE TODAY?

WRITE ABOUT YOUR DAY

TOP 3 THINGS ABOUT TODAY

1.

2.

3.

HOW HAVE YOU FELT TODAY?

WHAT INSPIRED YOU THE MOST TODAY?

3 INTENTIONS FOR TOMORROW

1.

2.

3.

PLANNING FOR SOCIAL EVENTS

One of the keys to long-term sobriety is being prepared. Social events, holidays and other gatherings such as happy hours can present numerous challenges to you, especially if you are new to the sober journey.

What leisure time, social events or holidays are coming up? What is your plan to remain free from alcohol during those times? Your plan should include being prepared to answer questions about why you are not drinking; non-alcoholic drink options you know will be available (or plan to bring your own); deciding whether to let the host know of your plans; and an exit strategy if you find yourself becoming triggered pressured or bored.

Event: ______________________________

Plan to remain alcohol-free: ______________________________

____

____

How I will answer why I'm not drinking: ______________________________

____

Exit Strategy: ______________________________

____

Continued on next page

Event: ______________________________

Plan to remain alcohol-free: ______________________________

____

____

How I will answer why I'm not drinking: ______________________________

____

Exit strategy: ______________________________

____

Event: ______________________________

Plan to remain alcohol-free: ______________________________

____

How I will answer why I'm not drinking: ______________________________

____

Exit strategy: ______________________________

____

Date: __/__/__

HOW WOULD YOU RATE TODAY?

☆ ☆ ☆ ☆ ☆

WRITE ABOUT YOUR DAY

TOP 3 THINGS ABOUT TODAY

1.

2.

3.

HOW HAVE YOU FELT TODAY?

WHAT INSPIRED YOU THE MOST TODAY?

3 INTENTIONS FOR TOMORROW

1.

2.

3.

ENABLING

Family and friends can be both a blessing and a curse on your sober journey. How will you encourage them to keep you accountable and not enable cravings you might have for alcohol? If your partner or spouse continues to drink, what tactics can you use to not feel deprived?

I can maintain accountability with my family by: ____________

____

____

____

____

____

When my partner or spouse drinks, I will: ____________

____

____

____

____

____

Date: __/__/__

HOW WOULD YOU RATE TODAY?

☆ ☆ ☆ ☆ ☆

WRITE ABOUT YOUR DAY

TOP 3 THINGS ABOUT TODAY

1.

2.

3.

HOW HAVE YOU FELT TODAY?

WHAT INSPIRED YOU THE MOST TODAY?

3 INTENTIONS FOR TOMORROW

1.

2.

3.

STAYING AWARE

It is not uncommon for other addictive behaviours to emerge when giving up alcohol. Frequently, habits such as shopping, working, eating sweets, playing video games or forming other patterns emerge that take the place of providing the dopamine 'hit' that alcohol once provided.

What other addictive behaviours might emerge when you quit drinking? Think about anything that could become obsessive and, long-term, harmful to your health, wealth and relationships. What strategies will you use to find and maintain balance in your life?

Date: __/__/__

HOW WOULD YOU RATE TODAY?

☆ ☆ ☆ ☆ ☆

WRITE ABOUT YOUR DAY

TOP 3 THINGS ABOUT TODAY

1.

2.

3.

HOW HAVE YOU FELT TODAY?

WHAT INSPIRED YOU THE MOST TODAY?

3 INTENTIONS FOR TOMORROW

1.

2.

3.

HANDLING DIFFICULT DAYS

Just as social situations and pressures need planning, so do those times in life when there might be hardships relating to health, marriage, work or bereavement.

During these times, a plan for self-care will be critical to your long-term freedom from alcohol. In the boxes below, describe how you handled a hardship in the past and how you would do it differently now.

PAST HARDSHIP

HOW I HANDLED THAT DIFFICULTY

WHAT I WOULD DO DIFFERENTLY TODAY

REFLECTION

Write down the changes that you see in yourself after quitting drinking for 1 week, 3 weeks, 30 days and so on. What patterns, if any, do you notice? As you look back over this journal, how have your moods and sleep changed for the better? What patterns do you notice in achieving and maintaining an alcohol-free lifestyle?

I have been alcohol-free for _______ days. I notice the following changes in my life:

____

____

____

____

____

____

____

____

____

____

Continued on next page

Date:__/__/__

HOW WOULD YOU RATE TODAY?

☆ ☆ ☆ ☆ ☆

WRITE ABOUT YOUR DAY

TOP 3 THINGS ABOUT TODAY

1.

2.

3.

HOW HAVE YOU FELT TODAY?

WHAT INSPIRED YOU THE MOST TODAY?

3 INTENTIONS FOR TOMORROW

1.

2.

3.

SOBER DATING & INTIMACY

Sober dating and sex can be awkward in the early days of sobriety. How will you dispel the anxiety or stories that you tell yourself about these experiences? What might you do to make yourself less fearful in these situations?

For each fearful thought, work through the following questions.

Fearful thought:

1. Is it true?

2. How can I absolutely know it's true?

3. How does the thought make me feel?

4. How does the thought make me behave?

5. Would I be a happier person without the thought?

6. What can I do to dispel this thought?

7. What is a more accurate statement?

Continued on next page

Fearful thought:

1. Is it true?

2. How can I absolutely know it's true?

3. How does the thought make me feel?

4. How does the thought make me behave?

5. Would I be a happier person without the thought?

6. What can I do to dispel this thought?

7. What is a more accurate statement?

Date: ___/___/___

HOW WOULD YOU RATE TODAY?

☆ ☆ ☆ ☆ ☆

WRITE ABOUT YOUR DAY

TOP 3 THINGS ABOUT TODAY

1.

2.

3.

HOW HAVE YOU FELT TODAY?

WHAT INSPIRED YOU THE MOST TODAY?

3 INTENTIONS FOR TOMORROW

1.

2.

3.

FINAL REFLECTION

When we remove alcohol from our lives, it is common to experience many positive changes. These gifts can give us all the evidence we need to never return to drinking.

However, some of the gifts of sobriety can take longer to arrive than others, and some can be totally unexpected.

Use the space below to consider what has changed so far, and what might change in your life without alcohol interfering.

Continued on next page

Date:__/__/__

HOW WOULD YOU RATE TODAY?

☆ ☆ ☆ ☆ ☆

WRITE ABOUT YOUR DAY

TOP 3 THINGS ABOUT TODAY

1.

2.

3.

HOW HAVE YOU FELT TODAY?

WHAT INSPIRED YOU THE MOST TODAY?

3 INTENTIONS FOR TOMORROW

1.

2.

3.

NOTES

Use these pages to make your own notes or where you need more writing space for the exercises.

NOTES

NOTES

NOTES

NOTES

NOTES

NOTES

NOTES

NOTES